T0208484

POETRY ON MY MIND

Tom Tenbrunsel

POETRY ON MY MIND

iUniverse books may be ordered through booksellers or by contacting:

iUniverse
1663 Liberty Drive
Bloomington, IN 47403
www.iuniverse.com
1-800-Authors (1-800-288-4677)

Cover Design by Erin Secretarski

ISBN: 978-1-6632-0041-9 (sc)
ISBN: 978-1-6632-0042-6 (e)

Print information available on the last page.

iUniverse rev. date: 05/06/2020

"I am amazed at what I don't know"

ACKNOWLEDGEMENTS

I would like to acknowledge my daughter Erin for her help and encouragement and patience with me in putting this book together. She has several other full time jobs, including, wife, mother of three, Asheville Reality, and competitive cyclist. I am so lucky she has my back. And I thank my beautiful wife and soul mate for tolerating writer's backside. Thanks to Abby Ruppert, Lori Smith, Erin Secretarski whose photos inspired my imagination to poetry. Special Kudos to Troy Carr for cycling into my soul.

FOREWORD

To the reader:

My poems are presented here in no particular order. I began writing poetry as a child, though printed documentation began around college. Retired now, I write more prolifically. My freestyle is short and intense. I cannot just sit down and write poetry. It comes to me, sometimes in the middle of the night and I write. Words and shapes flow from somewhere and I am intently immersed until the work is finished, the story told, the lesson learned. Every shape, word and comma are placed with intention to make my point. Photos are a part of my poetry, and I've been offering "Author's Notes" of late. I invite you to enter my world of imagination, thought, soul and insight. I would like to hear from you. Enjoy!

Tom Tenbrunsel.

NOTE: I have found often that I wish I knew what the author said about a particular work. I have included my thoughts and comments is a special section, "Author's Notes" in the back. I hope you'll find that section interesting and entertaining as well.

TABLE OF CONTENTS

BEGIN

FEEL

hear

see

smell

taste

THINK   E

SPEAK   V

DO   O

LOVE   L

laugh and cry

smile, joke & play

BE

DIE

TRANSCEND

Your Smile

Says...
"Hi"
Talk to me.

Laugh with me
love with me
live with me
come do with me

Touch me
hold me
hug me
make love to me

Smile with me
"what"

Your smile says...
I care
I want
I feel
I need
I am
in Love with you.

Giants in the Earth

Indians once roamed this soil

Great and hardy pioneers dug their faces in the dirt

In sweat and toil

Waste not for want this hallowed mirth

Giants in the earth!

My Love

My Love was only one month old,
My Love was scarcely two.
My Love is not yet three months old,
My Love I find is new.

But be My Love but ten months old,
Or nine times ninety-two,
I still would find My Love to be,
So New and True and You.

I Love You

My Heart

Be, my heart, be naughty
if naughty Thy must be;
But go and see the Lady
that makes my heart run free;
And, when you see the Lady,
kiss her, Heart, for me.
Speak these words unspoken -
say that 'I love she.'

All My Love

My love is so pretty, so lovely, so neat.

My love is beautifully close.

My love is cute with a smile and a wink.

My love is attractive from far.

My love is beautiful in Black & Bogue.

My love is attractive in pink, green or blue.

My love is lovely in pure woolen white.

But I see my love not as clothing (flesh) alone,

For indeed this does have its effect.

It is also my love, likened in God,

A God likened whole, and a personal person,

It is this, all my love, that I love.

It is this, all my love, that I love.

My Appalachian Unicorn

"Who?
What thing are you,
I've come upon,
In the woods,
    Whilst trekking?
Are you real?
I rather think knot;
Perhaps a fig,
        Or figment?

Then there you are,
Each time I pass;
To greet my imagination.
The Trail I take,
To greet you sir;
The Trail is Appalachian."

Twilight Morning

One morning just passed my Winter, I shuffled to the kitchen to fix me some "umm" tasty Chi Tea, just like any other morning. A bright crisp sunny day greeted me, cool to almost warming, a cozy early Spring on my mountain - new life, new chirping all-around, new sounds, smells and feelings. Dip the routine Trader Joe's powdered chai into a mug. Ahh, sniff an almost sneezy hint of that yummy, powdery, herby smell. Turn on the Keurig and listen to it telling me to "hit the road, hit the road, hit the road, hit the road," as it steamed up hot water. Smiling, I thought, "not today old man, not today." I pushed the brew button and voila - appeared a nice cup O' Chai Jo. I swear I remember stirring it with a clinking spoon. I stir my tea in honor of the Brits - in a figure eight leaving off the stiff pinky - not that boring circular swirl like the Yanks. It's not something I take for granted.

But then something strange happened. When I went to push the "off symbol," so's not to have it sit there fussing at me all day - nothing. Huh? It didn't work (I looked into the camera)! Okay, so push again and push and push, and push, push, push that darn little digital devil - nothing, still nothing? "What the heck," I asked out loud to myself, "I can't turn it off," pushing a couple more persistent, blistering times (hoping) on that fool fancy-assed off-tab? What's going on? Strange. Real strange? Stranger still - I didn't wake up that morning!

Solitude

Solitude is sometimes confused with loneliness
But it is Solitude that fuels the soul
In Solitude we are awakened
In Solitude we begin to appreciate
Solitude recognizes Love
In Solitude we confess our sins
Thoughts in Solitude, thank you Thomas
Solitude is the yen of yang
If a tree falls in Solitude, is it a tree?
Solitude proceeds words and is there when all else fails.
It is in Solitude where we hear ourselves think.
Solitude is to the soul, as Thinking is to the mind
Solitude is where we reflect – It is the quiet time when I realize really who I
am and come face to face with my imperfections
Solitude is patient and impatient
Solitude is the mirror of our existence
Solitude is the quiet before the storm

Listen to the sounds of silence
Solitude reminds me that I have something to tell myself
Be quiet my spirit, if quiet I must be
Be quiet my Spirit and listen to me.
Solitude is a fresh breeze
Solitude is fall leaves
Solitude is the falling snow
Solitude is a fire in the dead of winter
Solitude is a trout stream and no words spoken between kindred friends
Solitude like a thief in the night steals the angry soul
Without Solitude we are nothing, without Solitude we are not I
Solitude Stop – Look - Listen

Solitude is that deafening roar you hear right after you hear bad news
Solitude is the crickets and frogs in the night air
Solitude brings the silent frost that the sun kindly transforms
Shuuu! Quiet.

Solitude is the winged flight of the Owl
Solitude is the quiet before the storm – Solitude is the eye of the storm
Find Solitude and nourish it – Take a cleansing breath and relax.
Solitude is as near as your heart and as far away as the depths of space
where words have not yet reached
Solitude - Turn off the TV, put down the earphones and listen to nothing
Solitude - Read a good book, go fishing, take a hike
Solitude is that moment between prayers
Solitude is nothing and everything at the same time.
Solitude is infinite

Take one minute for yourself
Solitude is inner peace and inner peace must precede outward peace
Without Solitude we cannot proceed
Solitude is the path to the sixth sense

Cajun Christmas

Yuz'all MERRY CRISMUS WISH fvom all ov' us
ova' hyear ya hear!
Dis iz de day befo Crismus an' all t'ru my house
Dey ain't nutin hapn'n, not even a damn mouse.
De chirren iez all ova de place -
In Shecarago, Feenix and New Yoark or som'in place.
So's Mamma in her flutie wite gaown,
And i in mee garounteede cap,
I'z gonna selltle em bones down fo'
A long winter nap.
Ain't gonna be no clatter ov dem ole' gators on de lauwn,
Cause i'ma gonna shoot dem basterds ifen' dey do!
So wit a long pole-in stick
and a little flat drover,
I know i'ma g'wana bee a cajun St. Nick.
An' so up de chemin'ie i go,
Out to de flo,
Where i lan' wit' a splat!
(Don't recommin' doin' dat)
An' den turnin wit' a jerk,
Tell em 'gators toe git dem splashing asses on de move, i saiz',
"MERRY CRISMUS to Lisa,
"Til' I saw you some mo'!!!"

Ole' Cajun Sanna, by gum :)

Christmas Snow

Love, look at the window, how it's snowing.

10 trillion stars descending to announce His glory.

Slowly, Softly

all at once the Silent Night is white-black in possession,

Covering all

leaving none untouched in Love's obsession.

Majestically, Mysteriously

in the complex simplicity of each adjacent flake

lying quietly softly warmly fused

into the depth of one Snow,

To which Love will awaken.

Christmaslove

This comes as a wish at Christmas
Of happiness and glee,
To say "I'll be home for Christmas
To decorate the tree."
So I take this opportunity
And beseech our friends above,
To coin the phrase and wish you both
Many prayers and Christmaslove.

Oh Christmas Tree

Oh Christmas Tree!

Oh Christmas Tree?

What toys and joys you hide,

Discovered.

Old Christmas Tree,

An old man's memory;

Oh, Christmas Tree,

What Joy your Shadow tells;

The light brite, dazzling glitter; ✦

I fritter,

I Fritter away countless hours,

Mesmerized by your twinkling;

Wondering,

What Christmas will bring?

What gathering?

What Joy?

What Toy?

What Love?

What Child from above.

First Snow!

I sit alone, lonely,
Invisible in my chair,
Memory warmed;
While winter, suddenly cold and white,
Unexpectedly covers my earth.
When will it end?

The sun has abandoned.
I watch a red bird couple snuggle on a snowy Cypress branch,
Watching with me.
Is it their Winter?

Stillness surrounds me,
As nature swirls her blustery brush,
Renewing relentlessly with tiny flakes,
Reminding me;
It is My Winter too!

CHRISTMAS CANTATA

In a small country church where two or more or even more are gathered there is Love and there was friendly buzz in the air as people in the audience acquainted and re-acquainted, welcomed and good wished one another Christmas cheer, my dear bride at my side.

Carla stood up! There was sudden silence as she raised both arms, her back to the audience, commanding Devine direction, sublime attention.

From the corner, young college ivory began to move oh so delicately as if introducing a heavenly host.

Then boom! Without warning, in prefect unison, a wonderful explosion of red splashed heavenly voices filled the air, welcoming Christmas once more!

Notes soared, raised and filled the air, flitted, flickered, echoed, danced flooding every corner of the sacred room with Xmas* warmth! Then forever fleeting, but captured in this old soul's heart and tear.

There was a friendly cheer in the air as song and voice retold Emanuel.

The harmony as alto, tenor, soprano and sometimes base blended giving rebirth to Christ in Christmas.

My old friend was there among them, singing directly at me. Yes, it was jolly ole' St. Mick renewing this old temple, wishing me good tidings and cheer. The glue of friendship bidding an old friend goodbye and Blessed adventure for the New Year.

The musical web woven. The Xmas story almost complete - Suddenly?

Suddenly it was quiet. Unexpected and unannounced Kristie stood up approached the mic and with the clarity of a newborn angel delivered "Sweet Baby Jesus" like I've never heard it sang so beautiful before perhaps nevermore.

Through confidenced crystal clarity, vocal power, beauty, music and emotion, I understood Christ from Kristie.

A chorus mother a proud tenor father fought heartfelt pride, love and tears as they remembered holding sweet baby Kristie in their arms now a few short years ago in her own manger. I saw in their eyes age-steeled love for their angel.

What JOY a seasoned choir bestowed on us, mere mortals, that Christmas Seasoned evening. Music instills and heals. Friends are forever.

In that small country church God appeared, a musical miracle reborn –"Joy to the World, Let Heaven and Nature Sing, Let there be Peace on Earth, good will toward men."

*"X" is the early Greek symbol for "Christ" thus Xmas, Christmas.

From the Ashes

Alone,
In solitude,
In silent contemplation,
Instinctively reverent,
Not a ripple in the great pool,
Where once the Earth trembled,
And ashes lay strewn,
A boy stares at what was,
And asks his Mommy,
Who remembers,
"What can be?"

That Girl

He's met a girl
So neat is she;
I wonder if
They'll soon be three?

Ode to Thom

I feel inspired to write an ode,
To understand it you'll need a code.
Not the kind that needs a kit,
But the type that will fit
(The mood I'm in.)

Locked in because of snow,
I write this Ode to let you know
That whenever you feel blue,
"A friend has just prayed for you."

Victory is yours if you can find,
Every letter that is underlined.
You will see a message here
Whose meaning is very clear.

Schuelly

She Writes with Me

I sit and write my memoirs atop this ancient
mountain; a brook babbles below. A boy leaps
headlong into a leaf pile outside my window. The
sun is low in my sky and she writes with me

Message from the Chestnut

As sure as Frost upon the virus lay,
The Tree will stand supreme again one day;
Though time may toll beyond our mortal means,
The Chestnut will again adorn the country scene.

For lo, these mortals will come to plant and spade,
And cultivate the chestnut day by day,
And return it will upon this hallowed ground,
For it once was dominant and renowned.

But just as weak as we all are too,
So does the Chestnut keep growing shoots anew;
And its persistence is supreme insight,
Lest we not persist and shrivel from a blight.

Winter into Spring

A lone red bird looks at me;
Perched shivering,
    In a hemlock tree.
I look at him,
  Both wondering,
When the snow will end,
And will Spring begin?

Bluebells

Their color is like the clear blue sky
They hang like bells in towers high
Very early in the spring
I thought I heard a bluebell ring

Spring

Spring is as fresh as apple pie,

Flowers and blossoms renew,

See babbling brook,

Birds in the sky,

Daisies all new morning dewed.

The farmer plows, planting his crop,

Birds making nests in the trees,

New blades of grass,

Popping up from ground,

There's nothing like crisp springtime breeze.

Rocking

I sit on my porch in the mountains,
   Rocking;
Smelling the fresh breeze as it rustles,
   All but silently,
      Air unseen.
   My chores dun.

You'll find me rocking,
And watching,
And listening,
And musing,
And waiting;

Joe in the morning,
Sweet tea and a mater samich,
A brew at night.
Rocking.
   Pensive.
     Quiet.

Watching?
   Waiting?
     Listening?
       Rocking?
         For what?

"Winter,
   Winter, fool!
My Winter's coming.
Don't wanna miss it!"

Rock on!

The Road Least Traveled

I took the road familiar
And traveled ne're so far.
I took the road least traveled
And found who am, I are.

The Magic Bike

I came upon it rather,

by chance,

or was it destiny?

There alone it was upright in the woods,

beckoning

silently,

a lone bike eager for life.

To ride or not, was not a question,

for when I got on,

we coursed to parts unknown,

now "my bike" and me.

And I have never looked back,

nor been the same.

To my magic bike,

I gave the name,

Excalibur!

Biker's Solace

A lone figure,
               Dark;
A Silhouette of a man,
EnGulfed in thought.
Thought?
Of what was?
How did I get here?
What friends are these,
        That faithfully
            Ride by my side,
               Take care of me?
Of what will be?
What will become of me?
Me and my buddies?
Worry not,
For we are always with Thee,
        Take comfort, He,
            In memory.

The Tunnel

Into the tunnel,
     Unknown,
I willfully go,
    Willy Nilly,
Caution to the wind;
A double yellow leads me.
Hell-bent on,
  Decente'
What lies ahead
Darkness -
    And the other side.

Lost in the Woods

Lost in the woods,
Alone,
Quiet,
Life fading,
Stillness
   Invisible,
Darkening,
Strange and,
   Elusive,
But for fleeting glimpses,
   of my trusty steed.
Am I really me?
Homeward bound,
Yet at home here too!

Two Track

Something draws me down this two track. It's clearly a road less traveled. Who? What? Why? What's there? I can't resist. I must go. It seems to be calling me to my destiny, or perhaps to the end.

The End of the Trail

It was the end of the trail for me. I mean, I had been riding for miles, days, weeks, months, years. Oh hell, I have ridden all my damn life. I have miles behind me! Miles to go.

Suddenly! Suddenly, out of nowhere, on sandy soil no less, it ended! My trail ended. Vanished! It didn't just disappear, Poof! It ended nowhere. It ended dead end, in a brush of bushes, a thicket of scrub trees. A thicket so thick, I could not see the other side, nor even look back.

"WHAT THE HELLLLLL!" I shouted. "NOOOOOOOO! NO! NOT YET!" And just like that, with no plan, no pain, no roadmap, no warning (I was having fun exploring on my trusty steed) and just like that it was over. I laid my yellow beauty down and I was gone! I was on the other side. My bike I left behind.

Shocked? Hell yes! Disappointed? Of course. I was on a ride on the other side. I was about to find out, discover. Instead, "POOF," I was gone. I had left, unexpecting eternity. Damn! I had miles behind me; miles I thought yet to go! Disappointed? Uh perhaps, but then recollecting, I've had a full life right up to the end of my trail – and beyond a golden lake awash with a vivid sunset. Not bad. Not bad at all.

So come see me on the other side of the bushes. Come join me on golden pond, where the trail ends and life after life begins.

HAYDEN'S THEME

"She waltzed in, three, quite on her own, dressed so prettily, sat right down, determined, and began to play as if taught by some distant master.

She had neither lesson nor sheet, But she had posture and poise, no ounce of deceit. She had come to Play.

Ivory moved, it was as if the universe had suddenly sorted; It was time to linger, listen, muse, discover, celebrate and enjoy!

Echoed through an empty wooden chamber; "A" a single note rang out, Then another and another, perhaps one more joined in, then others;

Notes began to pour. They melded, flit and flickered, banged and flew; dancing with excitement, filling void with creative musical laughter and delight.

Was it middle "C" or the "B" beginning of a Symphony, "D" or perhaps a Child's Destiny, A destiny to create - Perhaps to paint the soul of Music?"

Love and Beauty composed of a simple score lifted the spirit of her newfound home. Every solitary note filled every corner with Joy as delicate young fingers plied a Rhyming Rhythm from that old box.

The Room came to life as notes appeared out of nowhere, crescendoed, swirled teasingly, flew pleasingly, then faded into memory, hidden now forever in my soul.

Then almost as soon as it had begun, it was over. Was it a Child's Gift? Of course. It was Hayden's Theme to these old ears and tears."

Leafy Leafy

Leafy Leafy way up high,
Like a leaf-pile in the sky,
Leafy Leafy come on down,
To my leaf-pile on the ground.

Tesser

I've tessered here.
I've tessered there.
I've tessered almost everywhere.

I've tessered in.
I've tessered out.
I've tessered here, there and about.

I've tessered up
I've tessered down
I've tessered all around town

I've tessered back
And tessered forth
I've tessered just for the heck
I'll tesser when you least expect

Tessering is quite easy....
You see
Come tesser sometime
With me!

Bucket List

Good Grief!

Today believe it or not I grieved getting old. And it wasn't really all that bad. There are good memories there's some things that have happened along the way, All in all I have no complaints. I have spent the journey with a good woman and have a good family and friends and have experienced life along the journey. I have no idea how long I will live but I'm okay with it. Is my bucket list complete? Hell no, I got a lot more living to go!

Stranded

1/2 between here and there - nowhere
Darkness snow blinding at a dizzy pace
I push forth in contradiction (unreality)
Brown's Lane - RR - and a sudden......
My head whizzes in dreamy unrealness
- silence darkness, I shut all power
in conservation.
I am panicked,
I'll freeze to death
Where to turn?
Only darkness.

Dizzily despaired in darkened desolation
Ditch, darkness, chains entangled and froze,
Red lights staring shouting,
"There is no power."
"There is no power."
There is no power greater than nature.

God
In the distance lights approaching -
A good Samaritan, his wife and their retarded daughter
Take me into the comfort of their home unassuming.
Kindness, safely and warmth,
There is no greater power than nature.
Thanks!

Winter Moon

Come shine in my window,
Charm the crooning, chorusing coyotes;
It is past brisk bright midnight;
All else is silent, still and quiet on my hill;
Bathe my soul in your solstice,
Free my spirit to rise to new heights,
For it's My Winter too!

Sniper

I have a friend
A cyclops
You don't see him
But he sees you,
Eliminating evil faces.

If I had a choice,
I'd clone him,
Who needs grunts
When he's up to bat
You bad folk
Remember that!
You best be wary.

No sound
No sight
Splat!
No heed
No need,
Your lights go out
With nary a warning.

The world's a better place to be
When Cyclops does his cleansing deed.

Air Warriors' Prayer

"We thank You, Lord, for these courageous young people.
We thank You for allowing them to follow their dream.
We thank You for the fellowship and nourishment
which we are about to receive
from Thy bounty,
Through Christ our Lord.

We ask You, Lord, to bless these Air Warriors,
As they go each into their separate "gray;"
Watch over them, and protect them,
As they travel on our behalf -
And their families.
We ask this in Your name. Amen.

To Lane Granite

What faces?

What Demons?

What Green Man have you captured in your granite clutches, Oh

Rock?

What have you seen lo all these million years?

And I yet just today discovered the essence of your tale.

Sprite

I have a Sprite,
That brights my day,
Wish I warn't,
So far away;
But when I visit,
She's the one,
That keeps this old,
Quite young.

"What thu hell you looking at, Banks?"

Mom

A butterfly haunts me,
Oft more frequently than not,
Flit and flickering about,
Quite boldly lighting on my sun soaked shoulder,
As if whispering in my ear . . .
Lovingly unafraid as I work in my garden and such.
She seems to know when I need her most,
And out of nowhere,
Fills my being once more
with life.
Mom!
Mom, "I'm here."

Good Morning Dad!

Good morning, Dad. You know it's really uncanny how much we look alike. For years, I never realized it. For I always pictured myself that little boy following in your footsteps, traipsing here and there, doing stuff with you together, just you and me. Now you're with me all the time. You were so much taller then; I'm taller than you now.

And we look so much alike with every passing day. I mean my face and knees and mannerisms remind me of you, even my humor and all those thousands of catchy saying, are ready on my lips. I even get out of the lounge chair like you.

I can see myself in you. I only hope I can live up to your friendliness, moral commitment, love for sports and God and family, your like-ability by almost everyone we meet. You instilled in me the skills and love for going outside. The kids are fine, your great grandchildren are fine (I can kinda see you in their upbringing). Oh, and your adopted daughter is so fine. She's still beautiful and has stood by me and you all these years.

Well, Dad, let's get another day going. You know, Dad, I never really knew it till Clint said it, but you "never let the old man in." I think it might have been your smiling personality and your careful planning of how to grow old. You knew you would someday not be able to get up and go outside. So you had your stamp hobby and music. You know, Dad, I still play that old antique banjo-yuke you recovered from your sister for me. What a treasure it has been for us.

You know, Dad, I'm kinda old now, in my seventies, and the older I get the more like you I get - and, well, you know, Dad, that ain't half bad! Why, your bedside table is still by my side (sighs!) and, yes, I wear a stocking cap to bed on cold winter's night, without the white elastic chinstrap (smiling).

Well, we've chatted enough, I got some writing and songs and a garden to tend to, just like you. Keep me in your prayers, Dad, as I will you. And thanks for the whole family and I thank you for being you. I love you . . . and with that, I turned away from the big bathroom mirror and went about my day.

A Nutty Story

A lone squirrel was looking for his nuts...
A lone hawk was looking for the squirrel's nuts too.
At the blink of an eye,
The bird swooped from the sky;
The hawk got the squirrel,
And the nuts!

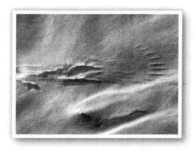

ALABAMA WINTER

Spirit Nymph

A Sprite, a butterfly, a Spirit,
A nymph visited my garden today.
I looked up to see such a sweet sight hidden
in amongst the vines and plants,
A beautiful nymph-lurking sprite,
"Well, hello there," I greeted,
And she didn't flit away.
But stayed to say, "Let's pick carrots today,"

"Why yes," I reply, "and some tomatoes, and okra,
A radish or two,
A beet is a treat,
And Annie beans too,
And peppers of all colors and hue,
And spices and herbs,
Let's pick them together me and you.
Let's plant and pick,
And pick and plant together,
Forever,
Me and you,
For you see,
It's your garden too!
You radiant nymph you!"

I was excited delighted,
To have her here with me,
The little busy bee.
We picked an planted till dark,
You see,
Then in a turn of events,
I vanished that night,
Leaving her here, My Sprite,
Alone In my garden,
No longer me,
The nymph,
my Spirit In she.

Moon

So open every window,
Throw open every door,
Let the moonlight shower,
Blessings,
Blessings evermore.

I am the moon remember,
Full bright up in your sky,
I was here when you were born,
I'll be here when you die.

I bring you summer solstice,
Your winter solstice too,
I rule your tides at sea,
I quietly spin for you.

I've seen famine, war and petulance,
I've seen muslim fighting Jew,
It simply doesn't matter,
Waxing, waning, full or new.

So sleep tight lowly master,
As circle you I do,
For one night I'll come to bid you,
Alas! your last adieu.

Strange noises, sounds and
messages abound around

The coffee maker says, "Hit the road" constantly,
While it brew's it's brew,
Then from the spout spews,
"Delight" to start my morn,
But does it also try to warn?
Is there a message,
Someone, something to inform?
Should I ignore?
And nothing more?

Then there was that midnight tapping noise?
I thought it was a visitor,
And nothing more,
But, then why would there be tapping, tapping,
On my night-dark window,
On the second floor!
This I can't ignore.

So I quietly slip from my bed, my ear to the wall,
My God, it's 2 am, and there's this insistent,
Persistent tapping call,
Tap! Tap! Tap, tap!
Like some mysterious,
Night-crazed, messaged McCaw.

What the hell! I've got vinyl,
Not Wood!
Tap! Tap, tap!
Go away you spooky, bane,
A bird insane.

What now?
The dogs next-door begin to bark,
Oriented to the gate.
Are they trying to warn me too?
Should I go investigate?
What the hell is it?
Could it be downtrodden Don?
And his meth brewing thugs,
Burying their evidential drugs,
Perhaps? – in the dark again?

Or is it that pesky, stealthy mountain Cougar,
Looking for my neighbor's cat.
I shine my 10 million lumen light;
Like a raging fire,
Blazing up the moonless night!

No one! Nothing to my delight!
Perhaps a shadow,
A shadow at my window's door,
Two glowing dots,
I close the shudder,
Back to sleep,
And nothing more.

The Old Storyteller Feller

Along the trail,
A brook and he,
    There he be,
Surprising me,
        By yon tree.
You knew he,
Miles behind him,
Had traveled here
From way aways far,
Perhaps along his way,
    Having logged in every path
And star.

I asked him for
    A story,
A tale perhaps of he.
I asked him to share a bit,
Of life's journey,
    With me.

He told story,
    After story, after story,
        And then more,
Nary one it seemed,
        I'd not heard afore;
Then like that, It dawned!
As he began his stories,
    Even more;
I swear that I had heard them,
I swear I'd heard before.

For he told how he had come,
By hookery
    And crook,
He told me of his journey,
To sit this
    Babbling brook.

Story after story
Turned fire-lit night

To dawn,
My heart beat fast,
Alas, now I knew;
The storyteller feller,
    "Was You!"

Yes! Yes, by God
I knew, I knew,
I knew, I knew, I knew!
Cause that Storyteller
    Feller
        You see
Was my Daddy,
    "He was you."

Many miles behind
    Me now.
As I trekked along my way,
My Storyteller, Feller
You see,
    Made me smile
        Each day.

A warm embrace,
Face to time-worn face,
My tear appeared,
    So dear,
To once more hear,
    Your voice,
And a story, more,
    Or two.
"I tell stories too,
Stories just like you!"

We had trekked along,
Some miles in life,
    Together, here and there,
    Him and me,
Missing him so dear,
        And him so missing me;
He had come back
    To trek with me
In my latter year -

As I had trekked with he,
For years and years and year.

He's come back,
Thank God,
    You see,
To see me,
Be with me,
    Once again,
To trek along beside me,
Toward my story's end.

Break Up

Sadly,
Heart-broken,
I lay in my bed,
Quietly,
Alone,
Late-night,
Grieving.

I am sad
    And yet,
        Somehow glad,
Maby it wasn't,
    Meant to be.
Did I break up with he,
    Or he with me?

Laying quietly,
With reddened,
Tear-soaked pillowed eyes,
Then,
Out from the Still,
A voice says maby,
    Just maby,
It wasn't meant to be.

With hope rekindled,
    In my heart,
I take a knee,
I have Faith in Thee,
And ask God, Jesus,
    From above,
Oh! I Hope,
Do send me someone,
Someone
    To Love ♥

Annie 7

She stopped,
Seven,
Hands on her hips,
And thru rose-coloured glasses,
Gazed upon her future.

They's are Ghosts in My Woods!

Holy Ghost!
They's ghosts in my woods,
They seem stealthy and quiet,
They're watching me though,
As I go,
    Invisibly white.

They seem to be moving,
With arms outstretched,
They seem to be calling,
"Come fetch! Come fetch!"

Every Spring it seems,
They seem to appear,
All dotted, about,
        Hidden,
Here and there.

For there,
They belong,
Hiding 'mongst leaf-less trees,
Seemly traipsing,
On fresh springtime breeze.

For, you see, they've,
    frequented these woods,
Neigh, many a' year,
From my good ghosts,
       You see,
You've nothing to fear

In fact, dear ghosts,
You mean so much to me,
To me, dear ghost,
you're more that a tree.

Dear ghost you see,
You're the tree of life,
Yearly renewed Beauty,
You remind me of Christ.

You see tree, your special,
For that Mark on your flower,
Your Dogwooded beckning'
                    That very hour,
That, That Tree saved our souls,
Eternally,
        Tree.

So carry on Ghosts,
You're welcomed here,
From yesteryear come,
To enlighten my forest,
With the message you've brung.

That men are saved,
By your ghostly reminder,
And you, ghosts, are free,
To forever wander,
My woods.
        With me,
                Eternally.

I Can't Find My Ghee!!!

Oh where, oh where has my little Ghee gone?
Oh where, oh where can Ghee be!
With it's taste so tasty,
And it's far fat free,
Oh where, oh where could Ghee be?

I'm lost, you see, without my good Ghee
Oh me, oh my, oh me,
Oh my Ghee.
My Ghee is the key to my cook-ery!
I cook with glee, with Ghee, you see!
That's why must I,
Find my Ghee!

If yee see my good Ghee,
Would you please call me?
I do hope you have seen my Ghee.
Did I hide my Ghee
In my pantry,
Or did you Ghee hide Ghee,
Ghee, from me

Everybody,
says stuff is tasty with Ghee,
And thinks the culprit's Nannie!
Tee! Hee!
That took the Ghee, Ghee;
But from what I see,
I'm gonna go
With the memory,

Of that culprit,
Tom T!

Well Ghee you see
Is biggern' a flea,
Even bigger than a bee.
Where art thou, oh Ghee
Thou can't hide from me.
And Thou can't hide from family;

See, Ghee,
They too love Ghee,
You see;
So A, B, C, Ghee
And E, F, Ghee, See,
Come out from wherever you be.

Poem by Erin, Nannie and Tom

CENSORED VERSE:
Little Tom T, has lost his Ghee,
And has no idee,
Where to find it.
He's in misery,
Having lost his Ghee
but he will make more you'll see
In the kitchen he'll be,
Dragging his Ghee-ass behind he!

Two Trackin'

Fun? Hell yes! I do this around western NC. Paved road went to gravel, gravel went to two track. Kept pushing through up down from Max Patch. Two track became overgrown bushes. You know when you have to choose between scratches from bushes and a drop-off you can't see the bottom of, hit ain't no choice. Then after ten miles exploring a new way to Hot Springs and my favorite Hot Springs Tavern, voila! We're Dead End lost! My daughter and I broke out into just enough room in the middle of God knows where, no still paraphernalia, no nuttin', just barely enough room to make a ziz-a-zagging turn around in my 2007 Honda Van and retrace forks after unfamiliar forks. Like Yogi Berra says, we were taking em! You see GPS don't work in these here mountains. And you mites'well forgot using that dad-burn cell phone up in here cept fur piture taking. It is a mite purddy upin' these hills and woods.

Well, we were a wondrin' what ta do bout now, when what do you know, outta nowhere God (cause it was getting kinda towards dark) sends a man and his wife in and old indigenous Ford pick-up. They squeezed up side-a-side, beside us on the narrow gravel. After a simple "Howdy," and chit chat, the rather pleasantly understanding man, answers, "Back on down a'ways, you take a right fork, then lean left and anudder left, then go about two miles and take a right at rattlesnake road. That'll bring ya rite out on the highway at Mumford Chappell." I turned to Erin, "You git dat? "Kindly?" And low and behold, after a couple a lefts and rights or so, darnit if'en we warnt at rattlesnake. We really warnt lost at all.

But you can get lost in these hear Appalachians, if'en you don't know where you are. Thank God I speak Appalachian.

Would I do it again? Hell yes! You ain't living, till you're lost along the two track backroads of America in whatever vehicle that brung ya ▪

When writing ends,
Reading begins.
When Reading ends,
Art begins.
When Art ends,
Music begins.
When Music ends,
The Story begins.

"What are words anyway, but an attempt to hold still – if only for a moment – that elusive, liquid quality that is life?"

Iris Chang, 3/7/93

AUTHOR'S NOTES

Giants in the Earth - Title inspired by Rolvaag's Giants in the Earth in my high school days.

Twilight Morning - Is the storyteller who you think she/he is and when, and more importantly, how did this work get written, considering the conclusion? Again, that unexplored space between life and death is addressed. Ask yourself, "is not death an extension of life?" Where does one begin and the other leave off? Or, in spirit, do we possibly remain? Does intellect and selfawareness extend beyond the grave? Are we allowed to experience the Chardanian transition of intellect/spirit? Which is more real? What can't you "turn off?"

I employed "foreboding" as the setup for surprise ("just passed" what?) Increase the emotional impact on the reader to quickly retrace and imprint the message. The setup for Twilight (Zone) begins immediately with "my Winter" continues through "I swear, I remember," and "Huh?," and culminating in "Strange" and "Stranger" (Who is the stranger - Rod Serling or perhaps Death?). When did I die?

I also try to get the reader to focus on their surroundings. Lose yourself in what is often taken for granted ("figure eight or circle") often glossed over or ignored. Life being short, I encourage you to savor every detail in passing, no matter how small. Does a coffee pot really talk to you? Really? Listen to yours. Remember what it was like to be alive.

In my work as a poet, I am reminded of the fine Appalachian American poet, James Wright. Wright (1927-1980) was elected fellow of The Academy of American Poets, awarded the Pulitzer for Poets, the Guggenheim Fellowship for Creative Arts and elected fellow of American Poets. Perhaps his most famous poem,

'Autumn Begins In Martins Ferry, Ohio' is something of a classic in the genre of deep image poetry. If you haven't read it, you should check it out. "Wright, in general, was a master of the compressed poem, the power to be felt in fewer words rather than more. For Wright every word, ever comma, every colloquially misspelled word belonged to the meaning. He, too, examined death many times over, and why not? This is what poets do."

To the writer do both, I encourage you to keep writing your poems, to keep developing your craft, your skill level with language and metaphor. Write from the soul, tempered by intellect and form. "This will have a positive effect on your non-fiction as well. You will see your language better as you loosen up, so to speak, to write your prose" - wise words from published author, friend and former Carl Sandburg Resident Writer, John Michael Flynn. Thank you, John, and write forever!

From the Ashes - Where once stood two great towering monuments, symbols of the free and enterprising world, another towering memorial stands now, along with a reflection pool and the names of those who perished. It is a memorial in honor and memory of what happened on that fateful day, 9/11/2001, there on that spot, on our hallowed ground. It is a place where people come together now, that we "never forget" that there is evil in the world and it is our duty to eradicate it with the help of God, in Whom We Trust. This photo of her son, which inspired my late-night poem, was taken by a friend of mine, 9/11/19. Friendships are a beauty of creation. They fill voids in the soul and make us whole. Friendship is the human spirit. The poem is a true story.

Sometimes I write seven poems a week; sometimes I write no poems a week. Poems happen for me. This one summoned up a decade and a generation of smoldering memories - A lone boy by the pool, our future, everyman. Daily I am reminded how fragile

Liberty is, and that evil exists in the world and how vigilant we must be. Let us pray.

Ode to Thom - A note written to me by my wife (Schuell), affectionate nicknames of newly weds.

Message from the Chestnut - Robert Frost wrote "Evil Tendencies Cancel" in 1936 predicting the virus (discovered in 1946) that "ended" the blight.

Spring? - Deadly Winter comes before Spring.

Rocking - The poem forebodes the old feller not wanting to miss his death?

The Road Least Traveled - composed with Biker Bill circa Team Redneck.

Biker's Solace - There is a hint of the Devine, mostly camaraderie and blessed memory. Dr. Bob, Big Bad Bob, sits exhausted alone among friends unseen, midway into a 40 mile ride out by Mrs. Master's place, The old abandoned Gulf station, just around the corner from the old one lane wooden bridge over the Flint River as it meanders along to the Tennessee. Aging, Bob's thoughts carry him to how blessed we are to have known each other and ridden many memory-filled miles behind us. It was God's two-lane Alabama backroads country - cotton and corn rows and us free-range bikers.

All dressed in black that particular day, BBB sits on the concrete abutment which once held gas pumps for motorist, since when there first were motorists. He stares at his thoughts, pondering dark - it's as if black represents the end of the line for Bob. Bicycles can be see in the background. There was a camaraderie unlike any other I had ever known among Team Redneck, a name we gave ourselves originally at the Hilly Hundred some three decades prior. We were a group of all ages, male and female, Team Redneck, some 100 strong, the oldest team in Alabama, with no rules, no dues, just come ride with us! Why did we ride? Because we could. I miss it.

The Tunnel - Life as we see it, with all its uncertainties, leads us down an unknown pathway, more directed than we think - a double yellow line controls us. The tunnel represents a passage, our knowledge of the future, where nevertheless, we unwittingly go. What lies ahead?" It could be anything. The old man is skilled, determined, yet destiny catches up. The tunnel has been his life. Life takes its toll. Happiness shrouds him as he plunges, irregardless of the uncertainty, headlong, consumed into the darkness that is death - in turn, leading him to the life, the light at the end of the tunnel, the other side, the hear-after, heaven, where his free spirit, freed, rides forever.

Lost in the Woods - I tweaked it a bit. And will put it in my "Book of Poems." Read the poem slowly, pausing to listen. It's about adventure, about life, about the beauty of being one with nature, about exploring who we are, about solitude, about the journey, about death and life after death. The rider likely had an accident or perhaps a heart attack, a stroke. Note the angle of the camera is from the rider's perspective. The bike, still there (waiting where he "left it" when it happened), the rider/writer, invisible now, writing (still a part of nature) from the grave? "Am I really (still) me," the writer asks, transitioning thru that unknown moment of life to death? Puzzled, exasperatingly rubbing his/her hands over her/his face and hair, the rider, "glimpsing" back at the bike (representing life's passion, life's journey), thinks aloud, "It, it feels so different - dead but, but still alive?" Where is the rider? Where is home? Do life experiences, memories, exist beyond death? Of course. Does a bear scat in the woods? - Tom, 3/11/2019

Note from John Flynn, Carl Sandburg Resident Writer 3/20/19
Nicely done, Tom. Simple yet profound, much in the vein of many short poems from the Chinese masters such as Li Po. The poem is grounded, not sentimental or false at all, and feels lived. You really cannot ask much more of such a form, and from yourself. In many ways, these are the hardest poems to write. You cannot afford to add one adjective or phrase that doesn't fit the whole. I am reminded of the fine American poet, James Wright. His poem 'Autumn Begins In Martins Ferry, Ohio' is something of a classic in this genre. If you haven't read it, you should check it out. Wright, in general, was a master of the compressed poem, the power to be felt in fewer words rather than more of them. He, too, examined death many times over, and why not? This is what poets do. Another poet you may like, who just left us, is WS Merwin. Both of these men were fine poets. We can learn from their bodies of work. I encourage you to keep writing your poems, to keep developing your craft, your skill level with language, your use of metaphor. This will have a positive effect on your non-fiction. You will see your language better as you loosen up, so to speak, to write your prose. I shared your poem with some Turkish colleagues. They really liked it.

Two Track - Much of my poetry is inspired by photos. This one was snapped by Troy on his mountain bike. He is exploring his new life. From the looks it's flat to the horizon, straight as an arrow, a sandy track much like what you find in a sandy State. It beckons.

How far does the road go? Past the horizon? Past the end? What's on the other side at the end? Does it just end and that's it? How far do you have to go? Can you turn back? Is it death or the journey that intrigues us? Where does the journey end and life-after begin? Am I already on the other side? Where are you? Where is that place for you? What is your destiny? Along what road?

The End of the Trail - The Trail of Life has limits. The life after trail has none. When do you die? How did the rider die? I don't know. I suspect rather suddenly, perhaps a heart attack, perhaps a coral snake. I leave that up to your imagination. When we least expect, the trail may end; so live life to the fullest. Explore, Love, Live and Celebrate Life, so when you die, you can say, "I lived!" Yet again, this author takes the reader through the transition (albeit fleeting) between life and death, between life and life after life. When you die, does the spirit just get up and waltz away - right through the bushes? Possibly. Does anything change in the process? Of course, the bike is left behind. Is life after life different? I don't know, but I rather think it's a bit like life before, and there's a golden pond (The original photo was golden).

Hayden's Theme - This prose poem came to me in the middle of the night. That day my daughter had messaged me the photo of her daughter, Hayden, saying, "Shortly after we had moved to Asheville, She just waltzed into the room like she knew what she was doing! She had been in her room putting on one of her prettiest dresses. And to my surprise, she sat right down and played the piano as if she knew what to do."

Well, I knew that she had not had a single lesson. I began to muse about the photo at bedtime, an often productive time for me. The concept swirled about in my head, haunting me, till I got up in darkness, switched on my desk lamp and put pen to paper. It proved serendipitous. Next day, my daughter sent the follow up video of Hayden's concert. It was magnificent! It was splendid, no banging, no discord from those mysteriously talent-laden, untrained three year old fingers. She called upon my mother's play-by-ear gift, as she began to make beautiful music - music I had unknowingly composed in my poem - the night before, before I had heard a note. I had captured exactly what she had performed in prose. It was uncanny, as if our souls were connected somehow through music. Although "Hayden's Theme" stands alone, I do have the video to confirm my poetic miracle. I hope you enjoyed my poetic/prose style

Leafy Leafy - Composed on the trampoline at 2212 by Lauren Elizabeth Tenbrunsel and her Papa,

Air Warriors' Prayer - I offered this prayer at breakfast at Columbus AFB the morning of departure for all graduates 10/23/97

Two Lane Granite - Along the Blue Ridge hike to Lane pentacle. How many faces besides Green-man do you spy?"

A Nutty Story - Look closely. The saga is imprinted in the snow.

My Spirit Nymph - Nymph? Yes. Real? Of course. She is my youngest granddaughter, Ann Hayden, still quite playful and interested in her Papa. She hugs me and I breathe in new life. She brings joy to my heart, you see. She reminds me so of Erin6! She's seven. I'm seventy seven. When she visits, it's Springtime just like the poem. Did I die in the garden? Of course. But my Spirit lives on, in those young ones who lift me up in my old age, for they are the who of the reason I'm here.

Mr. Moon - There is a man in the moon (the full face) and a woman's profile. They can be seen with the naked eye, binoculars help. The moon makes one revolution every 28 days, thus its "face" is always facing us. It has been Earth's companion since the beginning. The moon is more than a round rock placed there by chance. It is a monthly reminder of life and death. Sometimes spectacular. Sometimes eclipsing. Once in a blue moon is a long time, when two full moons appear in the same month. As the days grow shorter, the big full Harvest Moon appears and adds light at dusk to help farmers get the crop in as the days shorten. We

have been to the moon. The moon is an integral part of Earth. It is our heartbeat, put there by God.
Prayers.

The Old Storyteller Fella - You see here the bond of parent and child is forever. They did so many things together as they both grew up and old. Dad passed and so did time, albeit all too lonely without each other, but the memories kept them together in the spirit. There is foreboding, hints early on in the poem of what moment this is. Where will you meet your journey's end and who might be there? Will you be doing what you love to do at journey's end? A double negative belays the truth. He appears by "hookery or crook" from where? Did it take some finagling on the other side, from the Boss? Did he hike along a "pathway," a trail, in the "stars," in the heavens? Is he a vision, a ghost, a figment of imagination born out of the strength of emotion - or the energy generated by transition? Is it Teilhard de Chardin's "Sixth Sense," perhaps real in the moment? Perhaps life and life after life intersect? The narrator actually "talks to him." There is so much to say. But they have eternity to share. They "hug." It is real? Of course. Old, older now too was "she" (I did not identify her in the poem, so any reader could define the narrator, but this poem was inspired by a recent camping trip with my daughter, and I know exactly where that meeting takes place), and her daddy came back to be with her, to trek with her, much older now, on her way away. Lifelong, you hold the spirit of those you love. Did she too pass away, that day? Is there life after? Wouldn't it be nice if there were, and it melded with life before, on such occasions. Is there a heaven to trek?

Why do I write of such grief? Because the grief now is part of the happiness then. twt

Break-up - The Poem is of Faith, Hope and Love - the three virtues of the human existence I composed it looking into the future of

110

a young grandchild girl in love, I had, late-night, texted to sleep, from afar. And somehow it hit me. What will become of love. Some call it chance, others fate, still others coincidence. I call it Serendipity, the hand of God in our existence, intervening as if we were His only child, tending to us in every moment, sometimes without us knowing, fulfilling our life with grace and guidance. Thank God for God!

Annie 7 - rose-colored glasses in the original photo inspired my thoughts.

EPILOGUE

Through my faith and travels and in my many roles as spouse, father and grandfather, faculty member, university administrator, private practice, private business owner, volunteer, through sports and through my diverse hobbies and interests and adventures in life, I have had the privilege of meeting, sometimes becoming personal friends with, many interesting and accomplished persons. My parents gave me life and launched me into independence. I have been blessed by a truly beautiful and remarkable wife who has stuck by my craziness and travels and shared my journey. She is my compass, my rock. When the dust clears, she is my best friend. My three children, Kevin, Brian and Erin, have careers, have followed their passions and become their own persons. They have found wonderful mates in life and have given me the joy of eight uniquely grand, grandchildren, who are the reason for my existence. I continue to enjoy life and the continuing learning it brings to enhance my understanding of who I really am.
I thank you all.

"Such is Life, Such is Being, Such is Spirit, Such is Love."
                                                    - JD (Aspen, circa 1990)

Printed in the United States
By Bookmasters